A Little Birdie Told Me

Written by Jill McClelland, Au.D.

Illustrated by Ava Konton

I saw a birdie fly by me today.

She seemed like she had something to say.

I just watched her fly around.

But from her beak,
I heard no sound.

The little birdie talked
and the little birdie squawked,
but I just could not hear her.

She flew around me as I played.

She watched me
as I sat in first grade!

My friends could hear
the birdie sing.

But I couldn't hear
her say a thing!

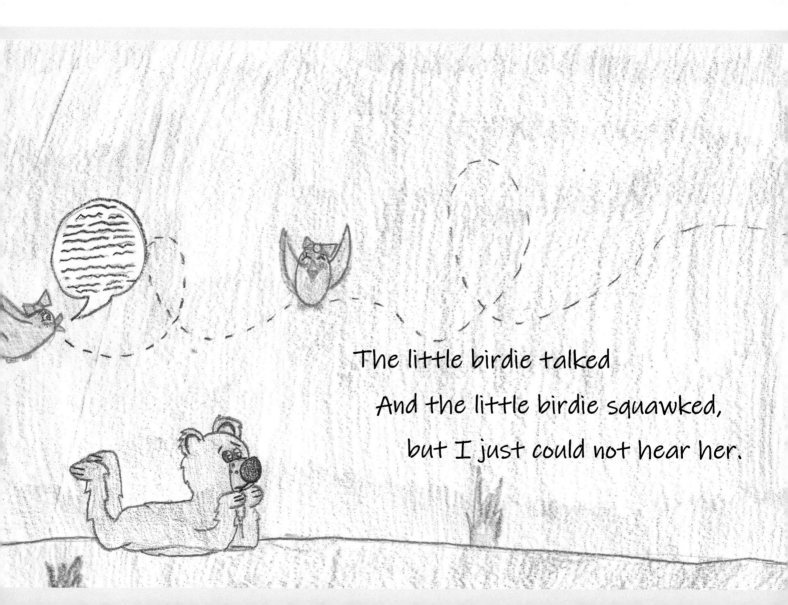

The little birdie talked

And the little birdie squawked,

but I just could not hear her.

I asked the birdie
why my friends were mad.

I heard no answer
and I was sad.

Just like my friends, family,
and teacher,
the birdie's too soft,
and I cannot hear her.

The little birdie talked
And the little birdie squawked,
but I just could not hear her.

And then one day

my mom came near

The little birdie talked
and the little birdie squawked,
and this time I could hear her!

Let's play!

I shared with my friends

and said many kind words.

The little birdie talked
and the little birdie squawked,
and now I can hear her!

The end.

Made in the USA
Middletown, DE
03 April 2022